The Ultimate **Chili** Book

The Ultimate **Chili** Book

Christopher B. O'Hara

Photographs by William A. Nash

THE LYONS PRESS

Guilford, Connecticut
An imprint of The Globe Pequot Press

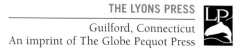

For *Maggie and Tucker, who like it with beans*

The Lyons Press is an imprint of the Globe Pequot Press.

Printed in Mexico
Design and composition by A Good Thing, Inc.

10 9 8 7 6 5 4 3 2 1

The Library of Congress Cataloging-in-Publication Data is available on file.

Contents

Introduction

When I wrote my first book, *The Bloody Mary*, I discovered the drink came as the unlikely result of the introduction of canned tomato juice, and vodka becoming available in France at around the same time. Lucky.

When I wrote my follow-up, *Ribs*, I imagined a similarly inauspicious beginning for barbecue—a caveman throwing the day's hunt on an open fire and gnawing at the results. So when I sat down to write this book, I wasn't surprised when I discovered chili, too, shared a rather unglamorous beginning: as a fancy form of pemmican, the dried meat cowboys would take out on long trail rides. (At least, that's one theory. But more on that in chapter 1.)

What do making Bloody Marys, slow-barbecuing ribs, and cooking up elaborate batches of chili have in common? There is no "proper" way to prepare any of the recipes; you just take a lot of different ingredients and mix 'em together. It's like that with Bloodies, barbecue sauce, and especially with chili. The best part is that you can't really mess up—you certainly can never find the "perfect" recipe. So if you love stovetop experimentation, this book is for you.

This book is not for the person who's going to the Terlingua, Texas, chili cook-off. That guy already knows a lot more about chili than the average person should. He is a "chilihead," a hard-core aficionado of "the bowl of red." This book **is** for people who want to be reminded of why they love chili in the first place, and are looking for some guidelines for their own recipe making. If you're like me, you'll discover that chili is more of an avocation than a meal. I hope reading this book is a lot of fun, and will help you discover the elusive, perfect "bowl of red."

Chapter One
A Brief History of Chili

La Dama de Azul

There is an old southwestern legend popular among chili aficionados about the "Lady in Blue," rumored to have written the first recipe for chili con carne. The lady in question was Sister Mary of Agreda, a Spanish nun of extraordinary beauty. Legend has it that she would go into trances for several days, awakening to report strange journeys to faraway lands where she would preach to savage natives, counseling them to seek out missionaries for their salvation. One of her more vivid accounts included a unique recipe in which venison meat, chile peppers, and onions were stewed with the fat of wild hogs.

Missionaries from South Texas reported tales of a strange and beautiful holy woman who traveled among the natives long before their arrival, preparing them for the teachings of Christianity. One Spanish missionary, Father Alonso de Benavides of the El Paso Mission, heard these stories and began showing witnesses a picture of a Spanish nun in a blue habit. Based on their reaction, it was clear the holy woman came from the order of Agreda, where the blue habit was de rigueur. Upon returning to Spain in 1631, Father Alonso discovered Sister Mary and heard firsthand accounts of her strange visions. She described in great detail the scenery and native peoples of southwestern America even though she had never left Spanish soil—surprising, considering TV and the Internet were not available at the time.

It sounds like a lot of hooey to me, but it's probably the best chili yarn around, and worth spinning a few times while you're in the kitchen with buddies waiting for dinner.

Pemmican

In doing my chili homework over the years, I frequently came across references to "pemmican." What was this strange meat? Luckily, I found the answer in the wonderful *Great Chili Book*, also published by The Lyons Press. At the risk of lapsing into overstatement, let me say that the book's author, Bill Bridges, has an all-encompassing, savantlike knowledge of the subject at hand. The man is a true authority. But as he himself points out, he is a distant runner-up to Everett Lee DeGoyer, whom he calls "the first renaissance man of chili."

According to Bridges, DeGoyer was a fabulously wealthy oilman who had plenty of time and resources to pursue his hobbies. Or, I should say, hobby. That hobby was chili, and pursue it he did, becoming—in Bridges's words—"a scholar of chili lore." DeGoyer was the first to postulate that chili was a uniquely American dish, originating from the common pemmican of the Southwest.

Pemmican (a Native American word from the Cree language) is basically fat and dried meat pounded together to create a compact, nonperishable trail food—one that can outlast a long cattle drive (or buffalo hunt, if you were an Indian). The addition of chiles to the mix, common in the Southwest due to the abundance of wild chilipiquin peppers, makes a logical and likely beginning for chili. In fact, Native Americans were the first true chiliheads. They would preserve freshly killed meat by drying it into jerky, using dried chile powder to season the meat and ward off bugs during the lengthy drying process. The reconstituted result was a crude precursor to the chili we know and love today.

Going on a long camping trip? Turn the page to find one of Bridges's spectacular pemmican-based recipes from *The Great Chili Book*.

Pemmican Chili

1 pound best-quality dry jerky, beaten until stringy and fluffy, or separated into fibers and chopped fine, or ground fine. (The first method is the best, but tiresome to accomplish; the third the least preferred. It takes away the character of the meat.) Up to a head of garlic may be added during the beating, chopping, or grinding process, crushed and mixed well into the meat.

1 pound beef suet, rendered
1–4 tablespoons crushed chiles, or more, to taste

Combine the prepared jerky and melted fat and mix until the consistency of hamburger is obtained, and the mix is equal throughout. At this point the only other ingredient needed to achieve true, old-time chilipiquins pemmican is the berrylike chile, crushed.

Always remembering that the pemmican may be eaten as is, or diluted into greater volume with liquid, the piquins (which can be found in many U.S. markets and in the Mexican food sections of some supermarkets in cellophane packages marked "chiles tepins") can be mixed into the jerky-fat mixture in amounts of 1/4 cup or more, to educated taste. Crushed red chile, like Italian peperone rosso, can be substituted for the piquins, but chilipiquins freaks insist the flavor (and hotness, remember) will be inferior to the real thing. Hudson's Bay Company pemmican was rammed into buffalo hide bags, called parfleeches, and melted fat was poured on top to seal the mixture in. The bags were then sewn shut.

Reprinted from *The Great Chili Book*, 1981, Bill Bridges, courtesy of The Lyons Press.

San Antonio: Birthplace of Chili?

The only thing almost every chili scholar agrees on is that chili (or, more specifically, chili con carne) originated in America, rather than Mexico, probably somewhere in the Southwest. Many speculate that the dish was an invention of the poor, born of necessity: The availability of wild peppers and the ability to use the cheapest, toughest cuts of meat combined to make a palatable, inexpensive dish. Most of the literature available points to San Antonio, Texas, as chili's birthplace—possibly as early as the late 1600s.

Back then, the Alamo was known as Mission San Antonio de Bejar and was populated by colonists from Spain's Canary Islands. Traditional Spanish stews were the culinary order of the day, and were probably flavored from local wild piquins. The mission's women would often prepare large kettles of this "chili" at home and bring it to the plaza to feed to hungry soldiers and missionaries. Although few accounts exist of the exact nature of the stew at that time, by 1880 these ladies were popularly known as "chili queens," doing a brisk business selling homemade chili at the Military Plaza Mercado.

At that time San Antonio was a bustling center for cattle drivers, the army, missionaries, and railroad men. The plaza was an open-air market, selling food during the day and almost everything else at night. The chili queens owned the night from a culinary standpoint, selling tamales, enchiladas, and chile con carne. They quickly became a San Antonio tradition, lasting until 1943, when sanitation laws forced them out of business.

Chili Goes National

Texas chili made its debut at the 1893 Columbian Exposition in Chicago. A few years later William Gebhardt, a German immigrant from the outskirts of San Antonio, registered Eagle Brand Chili Powder. The trademark was recorded in 1896, and the powder is still sold under the Gebhardt name. At around the same time, DeWitt Clinton Pendery of Fort Worth (by way of Cincinnati) started the Mexican Chili Supply Company and began advertising his "chilomaline," a chili powder made up of pure chile powder, oregano, garlic, and cumin. Advertisements for the product (which, incidentally, touted its healthy benefits and even claimed it to be a general curative for lymphatic disease, among other ailments) appeared as early as 1890, giving Pendery the historical edge. Either way, chili was slowly becoming a household name, and slowly making its way outside Texas.

By the early 1920s "chili joints" were found all across the American West. Known for their grubby, hole-in-the-wall appearance, these joints were nonetheless patronized by rich and poor alike, the customers drawn to the addictive qualities of a greasy, albeit properly made chili. Chili became truly legitimized in the culinary sense in the early 1960s by the famous Chasen's restaurant in Hollywood, California. Owned by Dave Chasen, its specialty was chili, which was widely consumed by some of the biggest Hollywood stars of the time. It's said that Elizabeth Taylor had several gallons of Chasen's chili shipped to Rome during the filming of *Cleopatra.*

Chili Cook-Offs!

Chili's seminal year was 1967, during which the first World's Chili Cook-Off was held in Terlingua, Texas. According to Frank Tolbert, the author of chili's official bible, *A Bowl of Red*, the cook-off was started as a way to promote the book, which had initiated a newfound interest in chili con carne. The idea was to get Chasen, undoubtedly the most famous chili maker of the time, to lock horns with Wick Fowler, the "chief cook" of the Chili Appreciation Society International (CASI). Chasen took ill right before the cook-off, however, so a replacement was found in H. Allen Smith, an obscure humorist who had written an article titled "Nobody Knows More About Chili Than I Do." In the piece, Smith insulted hordes of Texas-style chili fans by insisting that Texans didn't know how to properly prepare their own state dish.

The cook-off created quite a stir among chili aficionados of the time, especially Tolbert, who not only wrote what is largely considered the bible of chili but took it so seriously that he initiated the World Series of Chili, a cook-off that spawned thousands of regional counterparts over the years. Tolbert went on to found the International Chili Society, which held its annual official cook-off in Terlingua until 1975 (it moved afterward to California). The aforementioned Chili Appreciation Society International now boasts more than 50 local membership "pods" and oversees almost 500 cook-offs each year.

Chapter Two
Chili Preparation Primer

There's no doubt about it: The next best thing to eating chili is preparing it. And while the stereotype of cooking chili may be a mean, gruff-looking, bowlegged type straddling the back of a chuck wagon as he prepares a large cast-iron pot of chili over a wood fire, the fact is you'll probably be making the dish on your stovetop—and maybe even on an electric range. Here are some essential pieces of gear that will help make your chili-making adventures more authentic.

Required Equipment

A Big Pot

While just about any non-flammable vessel will suffice for the preparation of chili, it's usually prepared in amounts meant to feed armies rather than individuals. That means the larger your pot, the better.

I like to use a heavy saucepan or kettle that can hold 2 quarts of liquid comfortably. For that "authentic" touch, you can use a well-seasoned cast-iron skillet or Dutch oven. The great thing about cast-iron cookware is it retains the flavor of previous dishes, especially when used for sautéing meat. So

instead of scrubbing the pot out with soap, rinse it well after use, then wipe it clean—a small amount of natural oils will be left behind.

A Spoon

You'll need a spoon to stir your chili and ladle it out. I prefer a long wooden one, but it doesn't really matter. Have your pot and spoon? That's all you need to get started, unless you're aiming to become a true, hard-core chili aficionado. In that case, I recommend the use of some . . .

Optional Equipment

Mortar and Pestle

If you're ready to embrace hard-core chili making, you're going to need a mortar and pestle (see picture on opposite page). Looking like a miniature bowling pin (the pestle) and a small cup (the mortar), these tools are useful for crushing dried ingredients into a fine powder—chili powder, of course. When making chili powder, you can also use the mortar and pestle (or rolling pin, if you don't want to splurge) to crush toasted cumin seeds into a fine powder.

Blender

If you're preparing your own chili powder, you'll need a blender to purée dried chiles into a fine powder, and purée fresh chiles into pulp.

Rubber Gloves

Are you going to prepare your chili using fresh hot chile peppers? If so, you'll want to wear rubber gloves when peeling and slicing them. Surgical gloves work wonderfully, enabling you to manipulate the small peppers expertly while keeping the burning oil off your sensitive skin.

Meat Grinder

I'm not sure if you'd classify a meat grinder as an accessory only for hard-core chili fans—some would swear that chili made with store-bought hamburger meat isn't really chili at all. While I'd call that an overstatement, you may consider buying (or at least having access to) a quality meat grinder so you can select your own cuts of meat and grind them into properly wide proportions (more on meat preparation in chapter 3).

Hard-Core Versus Regular Preparation

There's nothing wrong with the way most of us prepare chili for a weekday meal. Fry up a package of ground beef, sauté some onions and peppers, add some spices and crushed tomatoes, and simmer. It's easy—and most of the recipes in this book are just as simple. But if you've never cooked chili the "old-fashioned way," you may be a little intimidated at how complicated it can be.

First, making scratch chili involves preparing the meat rather than grabbing a package of hamburger meat. For traditional chilis using beef, this means selecting a cut of meat and grinding it to the proper thickness or cutting it into properly sized chunks. Second, it means leaving the bottle of McCormick's in the spice rack and either preparing your own chili powder (page 25) or preparing your own fresh chiles (page 22). Like beans in your chili? That means soaking your own dried beans, another time-consuming process.

Obviously, you can make anything as hard as you want to. But making chili from scratch can produce results superior to anything you've ever tasted from a can or a restaurant.

Beans or No Beans?

This question is so volatile, many consider it the "third rail" of chili politics. In fact, more than a few Texas politicians have stumbled over this hot-button topic on the way to elected office and ended up in the private sector.

Chili has always been a peasant dish, its principal virtues being that it's cheap to prepare, it's a filling meal, and it's easy to make in large batches. I personally feel chili without beans is a bit naked, and apparently the U.S. Army does, too. With chili recipes dating back to 1896, the army fueled its soldiers on chili right back to the days of Teddy Roosevelt and his Rough Riders. In 1910 the standard army recipe for chile con carne included plenty of beans—mostly ground ones to mix into the dish as a thickener, and some whole ones to make the dish more appealing.

The bottom line on beans is this: Chili is just as "traditional" with them as it is without them. So have fun experimenting with different kinds (see Know Your Beans, page 29), or leave them out of your recipes to suit your taste.

Chapter Three
Ingredient Guide

Know Your Chiles

To be an expert chili chef, you have to know your ingredients. And by that I mean your chiles. Every other ingredient is secondary.

The chile pepper, the venerable plant of the genus *Capsicum*, is a member of the night-shade family of plants, which also includes tomatoes, potatoes, tobacco, and petunias (no wonder I like them). Chiles come from shrubs that can be either perennials or annuals, depending upon the climate. The American Southwest's dry, arid climate produces wild tepins, the small chiles popular for their pungent flavor and heat. Wider peppers such as ancho chiles are perennial plants that favor a tropical climate.

The chilihead consensus is that the chile pepper came from Bolivia, in South America, cultivated by indigenous peoples around 4,000 years ago, making chile one of the oldest cultivated crops in the Western Hemisphere.

The word *capsicum* is a derivative of the Greek word *kapto*, meaning, "to bite," a reference to the pepper's intense heat and pungent, biting flavor. Aztecs called the peppers *chilli* or *chiltepin*—loosely translated as "flea chile." However, chile peppers should not be confused with black pepper (a totally different species of plant, *Piper nigrum*) or bell peppers (the large and sweet peppers sometimes confusingly called capsicum peppers).

Chile Pepper Varieties

Chile peppers come in an astonishing number of varieties, ranging from fairly mild to emergency-room hot. Of the 7,000 different varieties available, nearly all of them could find their way comfortably into a chili recipe, but I'll limit our discussion to those you're most likely to find at your local vegetable stand or gourmet store.

Learning your chile peppers is as simple as trying them—you'll soon discover each pepper's unique flavor and level of heat. Here's a short list of popular peppers:

New Mexican

You'll see large New Mexican chiles in wreaths and ristras. Cultivated in New Mexico for hundreds of years, this chile is one of the mildest and most common in the Southwest. Extremely flavorful, with a very slight tinge of heat, New Mexican peppers are great for fans of milder chili—especially as the "base" pepper in a homemade chili powder.

Anaheim

These mild green chile peppers (also called long green peppers, chile verde, or Colorado) are among the most common varieties of chile pepper. You can order

them "stuffed" in many southwestern restaurants. Fairly mild in terms of heat, these peppers go nicely in some of the lighter recipes (Turkey Verde Chili, page 67), as they won't overwhelm the dish.

Poblano

More commonly known in its dried form as ancho pepper (*ancho* meaning wide). Fresh poblanos have a longish, irregular bell shape and, when dried, appear reddish brown. Their nice size and pleasant, medium-hot twang make them (for me, anyway) the ideal chile pepper. They are a great place to start your chile pepper habit, on the road to experimenting with the more fiery varieties. Poblano/ancho chiles are about a 3 out of a possible 10 on the heat scale.

Pasilla

These peppers are virtually interchangeable with anchos for chili making. Slightly longer and larger, pasillas have a dark black color and an aroma reminiscent of raisins (*pasilla* means "little raisin" in Spanish.)

Cherry

A small, very mild, round pepper usually found pickled. Not your ideal chile for chili, but it can be used as an attractive garnish or to add some color. Pepperoncini (sometimes called Tuscan) peppers are similar in taste and heat.

Guajillo

A shade hotter than cascabel and cherry peppers, but slightly milder than jalapeños, the guajillo pepper is one of the most popular in Mexican cooking. A fat, longish, deep red pepper with a sweet taste, the guajillo is medium in heat, making it an ideal choice for any chili dish.

Jalapeño

Perhaps the most popular chile pepper in the world, this stubby yet fat green pepper is a natural for chili. Yet as hot as they seem, among hard-core chile pepper fanatics jalapeños hardly rate on the heat scale. I find them plenty hot for the kind of chili I like. Making your dish hotter just requires using more of them, rather than a small amount of a truly fiery variety. When dried, they're called chipotle peppers. Fresno or guero peppers can be easily substituted for jalapeños in any recipe, as they're similar in taste and heat.

Serrano

This tiny, slim, deep green (sometimes bright red, when fully ripened) pepper is a great chili chile. A touch above the jalapeño on the heat scale, you may find serranos as dried japones, or "Jap" peppers.

De Arbol

Need more heat than a serrano, but less than a cayenne? Try using the small bright red chile de arbol pepper—one of my favorites for chili. Try substituting de arbol peppers in any recipe that calls for powdered cayenne; the tangier flavor will surprise you. The name *de arbol* (treelike) refers to the pepper plant the de arbol grows from.

Cayenne

You are undoubtedly familiar with cayenne pepper in its powdered form, which is fabulous for spicing up many of the chili recipes in this book. The chile itself is a skinny red pepper that's a trifle hotter than the serrano. Having these wonderful peppers so easily available in powdered form is a chili maker's delight.

Piquin/Tepin

These are the wild southwestern chiles of legend—and some of the hottest on the market. Piquins (or chiltepins) usually come dried, and are small, roundish, wrinkled, and orange-red in appearance.

Habanero

When you think of hot chiles, there's one word that comes to mind—*habanero*. Small, round peppers of pure fire, habaneros can be yellow, red, orange, or even white depending on the climate and soil they're grown in. Even the tiniest amount can give your chili enough heat to produce sweat on your dinner guest's upper lip! Use these peppers— and other extra-hot peppers—in moderation.

Heat

These days there are hundreds of different types of specialty hot pepper sauces on the market, each with names like "Insanity Sauce" or "Hellfire Sauce," all claiming to be hotter than the next. But how do you tell if one sauce is hotter than another without trying them all?

These sauces advertise their heat in Scoville units, a unique method of measuring a chile pepper's heat. The man responsible for the Scoville Organoleptic Test, as it's formally known, is Wilbur Scoville, an obscure chemist who measured the heat of chile peppers by diluting chile powder in water until the heat dissipated. Unfortunately for his colleagues, the only way to determine exactly when the concoction was rendered mild was to sip the fiery liquid, and continue adding water until a sip yielded a neutral result. When the pepper concoction no longer burned his friends' throats, Scoville measured the remaining water, and assigned a number. The result was Scoville units, measured in increments of 100. Scoville units go from 0 to 16 million, which is the exact Scoville rating of pure capsaicin, the chemical responsible for the chile's potent heat.

Scoville Units *

- 0–100 Scoville units includes most bell and sweet pepper varieties.
- 500–1,000 Scoville units includes New Mexican peppers.
- 1,000–1,500 Scoville units includes Española peppers.
- 1,000–2,000 Scoville units includes ancho and pasilla peppers.
- 2,000–2,500 Scoville units includes cascabel and cherry peppers.
- 2,500–5,000 Scoville units includes jalapeño and mirasol peppers.
- 5,000–15,000 Scoville units includes serrano peppers.
- 15,000–30,000 Scoville units includes de arbol peppers.
- 30,000–50,000 Scoville units includes cayenne and tabasco peppers.
- 50,000–100,000 Scoville units includes chiltepin peppers.
- 100,000–200,000 Scoville units includes Scotch bonnet and Thai peppers.
- 200,000–350,000 Scoville units includes habanero peppers.
- Around 16,000,000 Scoville units is pure capsaicin.

* Courtesy Graeme Caselton, Webmaster, "Chile Head" Web site. Copyright 2001. See page 99 for details.

Preparing Chile Peppers

The first thing to know about preparing fresh or dried chile peppers is that the oils and seeds inside contain capsaicin, the chemical that produces heat—enough heat to seriously burn the sensitive areas of your face, your eyes, and even your skin.

The key to safe chile preparation is to wear rubber gloves when handling them. When cutting the peppers, be gentle so as to avoid squirting the volatile oil into your eyes. And never touch your nose, mouth, or eyes. When reconstituting dried chiles, be cautious and use only cold water, as the steam from hot water can collect the oils and transfer them into your nose and eyes. Always wash your hands before and especially after handling chiles (even if you wear gloves). If your skin starts burning, try washing your hands with a paper towel moistened with clear vinegar.

Always choose chiles that are mature, heavy for their size, and smooth. Chiles that appear shriveled or bruised should be avoided, as should chiles that are overly wrinkled. Picking fresh chile peppers is similar to selecting regular bell peppers; you are looking for a "crisp" appearance and, preferably, a pepper that is slightly underripe.

I always buy my chiles in large batches, mainly because I live in the Northeast, and you never know when a reliable batch of fresh peppers is going to make its way to the local specialty food store. That means purchasing them in bulk and freezing them. There is a certain amount of work involved in preparing and storing them, but the end result is that you are always prepared to make the freshest chili. Here's what you should do.

Begin by removing the outer skin from your chiles. This is fairly simple. First, thoroughly wash and dry the chile. Poke a slit in the side of the chile to allow steam from the moisture inside to escape. Next, use a heat source to burn the outer layer of the pepper. This is called blistering. I usually set my oven's broiler at 500 degrees and place the chiles on a baking sheet, close to the heat source (gas is preferred, but electric coils do a good job). Turn them every minute or so, until the entire outer layer has a blistered appearance. This should take as little as 5 minutes. Another method is to blister them directly over a grill (your outdoor grill, or by means of a wire-mesh grill placed over a gas burner on your stove). It really doesn't matter how you accomplish the task—I have even used a small butane torch, held several inches away from the skin (this is like caramelizing sugar on top of a crème brûlée).

Now that your chiles are blistered, allow them to cool off. The skin should separate easily. I actually prefer dunking chiles into ice-cold water immediately after blistering—it helps retain color and makes them crisper. Once you have removed the blistered skin, take a small knife and remove all seeds and stems from the peppers. Seal the chiles well, using plastic bags or other sealed containers (remove the air first), and place them in the freezer. The prepared chiles can be sliced frozen and cooked without defrosting.

Reconstituting Dried Chiles

These days you can find a large variety of dried chiles at your local gourmet store, supermarket, or over the Internet. I recently bought packaged chiles from a company called Chile Today, Hot Tamale at my local natural food store and was surprised at the variety (nearly a dozen different types, including hard-to-find piquins) and quality.

When you find a good supply of dried chiles, it's good to stock up—they won't go bad. Reconstituting the peppers is as simple as boiling them in water for about 10 minutes. After they have regained their softness and pliability, set them aside to cool and dry. Slit them down the middle and remove seeds and stems, being careful to wear gloves when handling the hotter varieties. You can then chop the stemmed and seeded chiles and add them directly to the recipe, or purée them in a blender. Don't forget to reserve some of the water you boiled the chiles in; it retains a tremendous amount of flavor and heat. A cup of pepper water can be used to thin down an overly thick chili, while adding some heat and pungency. Be extremely careful when reconstituting really hot peppers, such as habaneros, Scotch bonnets, and Thai chiles. The volatile oils can easily catch a ride aboard the steam and get into your nose and eyes.

Chili Powder

Thanks to the aforementioned Misters Gebhardt and Pendery, we don't have to go through the time-consuming process of peeling hot peppers in order to prepare a world-class chili. Chili powder—really a mix of dried chiles, cumin, garlic, and

oregano—probably shaves a good hour off traditional chili preparation, and the results are just as tasty.

Back in the heady days of the late 1800s, there were many southwestern cooks who pooh-poohed the new powders, believing them to be an inferior substitute for the "real thing." Those cooks were probably also using Pendery's patented "chilomaline" on the sly. The fact is, there is nothing better—or simpler—than preparing chili using powder. Of course, it depends on the powder.

Most American spice racks include a jar of McCormick's chili powder on the lazy Susan. Great for dry-rubbing ribs, seasoning taco meat, and making barbecue sauce, chili powder has become a staple of the American spice cabinet—even though most people couldn't tell you what's in it! To be a proper chili aficionado, you have to know your peppers. But you also have to know your powder. A great way to learn about chili powder is to prepare your own.

Make Your Own Chili Powder

Making chili powder for the first time is sort of an exercise in demystification. For many years, you've probably liberally sprinkled your McCormick's over ground beef with little regard to what, exactly, was inside the jar. When you actually prepare your own, you'll be amazed to see how easy it actually is. You'll also be one of the few people who know the secret ingredients, and be able to brag about it for years to come.

Before you start, you should have a winking familiarity with chile peppers. Making chili powder may be a crude and simple alchemy, but try making one with just cayenne and Scotch bonnet peppers, and you'll be making bug repellent rather than spice! I have suggested a "basic" type of recipe below—one that you can use as a base to experiment with, adding or subtracting various ingredients to adjust for flavor and heat. Start by assembling the following:

> 8 dried poblano chiles (called anchos, remember?)
> 8 dried Anaheim chiles (substitute New Mexican or Cubanel)
> 6 dried chipotle chiles (smoked and dried jalapeños)
> 1/4 cup cumin seeds, toasted
> 1/4 cup garlic powder
> 4 teaspoons ground oregano

The first step is to toast the chiles. You'll notice that the "dried" chiles you're using are still fairly moist and pliable. To toast them, slice them in half and remove the stems and seeds (as discussed above, remembering to wear rubber gloves). Heat your oven to

300 degrees and place the sliced chiles on a baking sheet for approximately 5 to 10 minutes. Be sure to check on them periodically, as the larger chiles will take longer to toast. You can remove the smaller ones from the oven as you go. When done, place the toasted chiles in a blender and pulse them on the highest setting for a few seconds. Remove the powder from the blender and set it aside.

Now it's time to toast your cumin seeds. (You can buy prepared cumin powder, of course, but since you're going through all the trouble, you might as well do it right!) Using a dry skillet over medium heat, toast the cumin seeds until they are several shades darker in color—about 5 minutes. Use either a mortar and pestle or a rolling pin to crush them. When using a rolling pin, place the toasted seeds between two pieces of waxed paper and proceed to bash them liberally until they are powdered. This is by far the most difficult part of the whole process—but it's worth it, because there's nothing more flavorful than fresh cumin powder!

The rest is simple: Put the cumin powder, chile powder, garlic powder, and oregano into the blender and pulse until well mixed. You now have approximately 2 cups of authentic chili powder.

Now the fun begins. Want a really hot powder? Try taking away 1 poblano and adding a few Scotch bonnets or a cayenne pepper. Want something more mild and flavorful? Subtract 3 chipotles, replacing them with more flavorful New Mexican chiles. You get the idea. You can store chili powder indefinitely, provided that you use a dry, sealed container. I like to use empty McCormick's or Spice Island jars for keeping a limited supply of powder close at hand, and save the rest in well-sealed bell jars.

If you come across a really good supply of a particular chile, you may want to toast the whole batch and make it into powder without adding the oregano, garlic powder, and cumin. When you have a variety of the raw ingredients at hand, there's nothing more fun than experimenting right at the pot while you're cooking. This way, you can throw in a teaspoon of ancho powder here, a bit of chipotle powder there, and mix things up at will. You can use fresh garlic and oregano if you want, and be able to adjust the level of flavoring and heat as you cook. Or you can just stick with the McCormick's and use your special powdered chiles to doctor it up! But be warned: After making your own chili powder even once, you'll always feel like you're "cheating" a bit when you use the supermarket variety.

Know Your Beans

As far as I'm concerned, there's nothing more unsettling than chili without beans. I'm going to have to take a stand on this hot-button chili issue—even if it means alienating half my audience. However, I respect the other half's opinion; I've had dozens of bowls of beanless chili and enjoyed them to the last spoonful. Since beans are the final ingredient added to a chili concoction, you can ponder up to the very last minute whether to include them or not. But if you're going to be making chili with beans, you ought to know something about them. Here's a brief but informative overview.

Canned Beans

Most of the time you're going to grab a few cans of Goya beans at the supermarket and call it a day. That's what I usually do, and I've yet to hear a complaint. The international foods section of your local market has plenty of canned beans to choose from, including almost every variety that you could possibly put in a batch of chili.

When using canned beans, pour them into a colander and thoroughly rinse them, getting rid of the viscous packing syrup. Add canned beans about 15 minutes before the pot of chili is done. They tend to be somewhat mushy from the can and, hence, more prone to breaking apart during the cooking process. Unless you're making army chili, you'll want your beans as pristine as possible. Whole unblemished beans add a fantastic visual dimension to chili with their shapes and colors. They also add texture—a critical aspect of the perfectly balanced chili dish.

Dried Beans

Chili pros like to prepare their own fresh chiles (or make their own custom chili powder), grind their own meat, and toast their own cumin, all of which I've described above. But most important, they like to use dried beans. Now, when I'm faced with the choice of canned or dried, canned beans are going to win out 90 percent of the time; they're infinitely easier to prepare. So why would anybody take the time to buy dried ones?

Most of the world still buys its beans dried. Dried beans are not only cheaper than canned beans, they're also a lot more fresh and flavorful. They store more easily, and you can use exactly as much as you need, rather than wasting a whole can when you need only half as much.

Soaking Beans

When preparing dried packaged beans, you should soak them before cooking for two reasons. First, soaking the beans brings back their natural water content, making them softer. Second, the chemicals that cause beans to be widely known as the "magical fruit" (the more you eat, the more you toot) are displaced.

For 1 cup of beans, add 5 cups of hot water, remembering that during the soaking process the beans will expand to about triple their size during the soaking process. Be sure to have a large-enough pot. Soaking them with hot water will take about 2 hours. If you are in a rush, you can cut the time in half by boiling the beans for 2 to 3 minutes then turning off the flame, allowing them to soak in a covered pot. Don't use the water you soaked the beans in for cooking.

Cooking Beans

The key to cooking beans is to get them tender without making them mushy. And unless your beans have been supplied by the World Bank, a bag of dried beans should have detailed cooking instructions on the package. It's wise to follow them, as beans can vary in cooking time from 30 minutes to 2 hours.

Here's the basic drill: Place your soaked, well-rinsed, and drained beans in a large water-filled saucepan (use new water, not the soak water), so that the beans are covered by approximately an inch of water. Add a tablespoon or two of oil, just as you would for cooking pasta, to keep boil-overs and stickiness to a minimum. Boil them for about 10 to 15 minutes, and then reduce the heat to a simmer and cook until tender. It depends on the bean, so consult your directions. For chili, I like to take my beans out about 15 minutes before they are done, and let them finish cooking in the chili (which means adding them to your chili about 15 minutes before it's done). That gives the beans a chance to get seasoned and will ensure a tender, rather than mushy, bean.

Bean Varieties

Here's a short list of classic beans for chili:

Pinto

Often used for refried beans, pintos have an earthy flavor but a light texture. When using cooked pintos in chili, be sure to add them at the last minute, or they'll become mushy. Pintos take about 2 hours to cook.

Navy

Also known as pea beans, navy beans are most often found in pork and beans. They are an excellent chili partner, as they hold up well and add great texture and subtle flavor. Cook them for about 1½ to 2 hours.

Black

My favorite chili bean, the venerable black bean (*frijole negro*, if you speak Spanish) is the staple of many a Latin American diet. Black beans are the perfect chili companions, and take a little over an hour to cook.

Dark Red Kidney

This is the larger sister of the *frijole negro* in terms of its chili heritage. You won't find these dried, only in cans. Known as the Mexican bean, kidney beans are the number-one chili bean, and for good reason. They are a good size, have a wonderful flavor, and provide a tender texture that goes perfectly with meat.

Pink

The tiny, pale pink bean packs a tremendous amount of flavor for its size. It's a close cousin to the kidney bean and cooks in just under an hour.

Small Red

Also called the Mexican red bean, small red beans are perfect for chili, stews, and Creole dishes. Basically a smaller version of the dark red kidney, small red beans are a great choice for chilis with lots of ingredients, because they do not dominate the bowl as larger beans can.

Light Red Kidneys

For some strange reason, these tend to have a richer flavor than the dark red kidney beans, with a soft, appealing texture that's perfect in chili. They are also known as Mexican beans.

Essential Spices

Most of the spices you need to make chili are found in chili powder: chiles, garlic, cumin, and oregano. For any of the recipes in this book that call for fresh chiles, you'll want to have all of the components available separately, as well as a few more.

Chile Powder

No, not *chili* powder, *chile* powder. I don't expect anybody other than hard-core aficionados to have jars of various powdered chiles available to them. If you do, you can have a lot of fun experimenting with various doses to vary the flavor and heat of your chiles. I keep a generous-sized jar of habanero powder on hand, using it just as I would cayenne pepper—to add heat and peppery flavor to my chili recipes.

Cumin

Whether toasted in the pan and then hand-ground or store-bought in its powdered form, cumin is one of the essential chili spices. Cumin is just at home in tamales, enchiladas, and chili as it is in meat loaf. An ancient spice, cumin is also known as *comino* and hails from India. Use it liberally.

Garlic

Garlic is second only to the chiles themselves as an essential chili ingredient. Try having chili without garlic, and you'll be sorely disappointed. Even

though powdered garlic is a key component of chili powder, you'll often sauté fresh garlic in the skillet before adding meat, infusing flavor throughout the long cooking process. If you have to use prepared garlic powder in your recipes, use it sparingly—it has a much more pungent flavor than fresh garlic.

Oregano

Oregano found its way into chili via Mexico, where it was used to flavor stews and meats. Although widely embraced by southwestern chiliheads of the time, it's rumored that the herb didn't gain popularity until World War II, when soldiers stationed in Italy came back to the States with the newly acquired taste.

Other Spices

Using just the four spices listed above (chiles, garlic, cumin, and oregano), you'll be able to make award-winning chili. But there are a whole lot more "secret" and "special" ingredients a chili cook can add. I would never be able to detail all of the spices that have found their way into my chili pot over the years, but I can suggest a few key spices that have appeared in more than one blue-ribbon chili recipe.

Cayenne Pepper

If you read the section on chiles, you'll know that the bottled cayenne pepper you have in your spice rack bears no resemblance to black pepper—which is actually *Piper nigrum*, a different species of pepper altogether. Cayenne pepper is merely powdered cayenne peppers. If you're like most people, you'll be happy to use the premade powder, instead of going through the hassle of peeling, toasting, and powdering fresh peppers.

Red Pepper Flakes

Yep, the kind you use on pizza. Kind of a poor man's chile pepper, you can add some to your friend's bland chili to give it a lift. Hot pepper flakes are merely bits of dehydrated hot chile peppers.

Adobo

A clever mix of onion powder, salt, garlic, oregano, and monosodium glutamate, adobo has been the "secret" ingredient in many a chili over the years. Like it or not, MSG does magical things to chili, acting almost as a flavor booster. Remember to ask your friends if they're allergic first (even though I've never served anybody at my dinner table who was).

Sugar

The best chilis often strike the perfect balance between spicy and sweet. The sweetness in chili can come naturally, through natural sugars in vegetables like onions, or it can be added. While a tablespoon of white granulated sugar will usually suffice, there are a variety of cool ways to sweeten your chili. My friend Tim Coleman turned me on to a healthy dose of Vermont maple syrup, added about 15 minutes before the pot is done. Another friend swears by brown sugar, as do many other well-known chili chefs. Still others use a small dose of honey or molasses.

Salt and Pepper

Both salt and pepper are called for to properly season chili. At the risk of insulting your culinary intelligence, I will caution you to use both sparingly—especially if you are using a canned chicken broth (already loaded with sodium) or an abundance of chile peppers (spicy enough)! There's nothing better than spicy chili, but there's nothing worse than an *overly* spicy chili (hence the many and varying antacid commercials citing chili as a source of gastric discomfiture).

Herbs

At the risk of making chili purists cringe, I will mention a few herbs that mix comfortably in most chili dishes. You won't see any hombres in 10 gallon hats mixing these into a bowl of red, but marjoram, dill, rosemary, sage, and coriander can all blend comfortably into any of the recipes in this book.

Paprika

Making chili without tomatoes, and need to add a convincing dose of color to your bowl of red? Paprika's the answer. Another member of the *Capsicum* genus, in its American form paprika is a mild powdered pepper. The Hungarian variety is seriously spicy, and the principal ingredient in a good goulash. Use the familiar kind to add color (rather than flavor) to plain brown chilis that need dressing up. If you can find the spicy Hungarian variety, you can substitute it for cayenne pepper.

Meat Grades

Believe it or not, there are eight different quality grades of beef. Unless you happen to be in the meat business, you are probably familiar with only the top three: "prime," "choice," and "select." It makes you wonder what the other five categories are called, doesn't it? So what's the difference between the three grades, and what is the proper grade to select for chili?

"Prime" meat is considered the top grade in the United States. Produced in limited quantities, prime meat is generously marbled with veins of fat which makes it very tender. The top cuts of rib-eye, sirloin, T-bone steaks, and filet mignon are divided from the more proletarian cuts and distributed to restaurants and specialty meat markets or shipped overseas. At prices approaching $10 for one medium-sized rib-eye steak, prime meat can be a luxury. Prime meat makes for great steaks, but lousy chili (unless you do it right—see page 64 for the Grilled Rib-Eye Chili recipe).

"Choice" meat comes next. These are the cuts that make it to your local supermarket. There's nothing wrong with choice steaks, but this type of meat shouldn't see the inside of a chili pot—the more tender, fatty cuts of meat just won't hold up under several hours of cooking. When you think of a great steak, you like to say that the meat just "melts in your mouth." That's exactly the type of meat you want to avoid in chili cooking.

"Select" meat (kind of akin to calling a janitor a "hygienic consultant") is cheap meat. Yep, we're talking end cuts here: brisket, round, roasts, and so on. This is chili meat— nice and lean, and pretty tough. The key is knowing how to coax the proper flavor and texture out of the meat during the process of cooking chili. With chuck meat, you don't have to worry about choosing "choice" over "select." In fact, the less expensive select variety is far better, as it will have significantly less fat.

Meat: Chili Cuts

The proper cut of meat for chili comes almost exclusively from the "chuck" family. *Chuck steak* encompasses top-blade, shoulder, arm, chuck-eye, mock tender, and seven-bone steak. These cuts are more commonly called London broil, shoulder steak, bottom chuck, and center chuck. Confused? Don't worry about it; just make sure you get chuck meat in the familiar pot roast style—the leaner the better.

Chili meat requires no special preparation—no marinating, no dry-rubbing. It does, however, need to be cut into pieces large enough to withstand a long cooking process and vigorous stirring. Use the term *bite sized* as your guide—cubes no smaller than ¼ inch and no larger than ½ inch. If you are going to grind your own chili meat, use the largest plate your grinder provides—the one with holes about the diameter of your pinkie.

I won't lie to you and say that every time I cook chili, I slice or grind my own chuck meat. The truth is, there's often a lonely frozen package of hamburger meat (ground chuck) that gets called into service. Ground chuck, while convenient, doesn't make a top-quality chili. It's far too mushy, and way too fatty. Take the extra time to either have your butcher grind fresh chuck steak into the proper size or cube a chuck roast and slow-simmer it. I promise it will be worth the extra effort.

Of course, you can safely substitute hamburger meat in every single one of the beef recipes in this book, and probably be fairly pleased with the results. Just be sure to reduce the cooking time; the whole point of cooking chili slowly is to tenderize the meat.

Chili Additives

Everyone who's serious about making chili has a "secret" ingredient. Mine is Hershey's Cocoa, the old-fashioned chocolate baking powder. I put a heaping tablespoon of it into a quart of chili, and it does something magical. Others swear by a dollop of maple syrup. Margo Knudson, the 1987 ICS World Chili Champion, uses an undisclosed amount of "oregano tea" in her award-winning recipe. Jim Beaty snuck ½ tablespoon of MSG into his "Sespe Creek Chili" and took away the 1986 ICS crown. Will anyone really notice a dollop of secret ingredient hidden in 2 quarts of extra-spicy chili? Maybe, maybe not, but here are some of the additives that can turn an ordinary bowl of red into your own "secret recipe":

Beer

Beer has been a key ingredient in many an award-winning concoction over the years. Budweiser seems to be the beer of choice among serious chili connoisseurs. Try substituting beer in recipes that call for a cup of water or broth.

Mole

Mole (pronounced "mole-ay") is a rich Mexican sauce generally made from onion, garlic, chiles, ground nuts, and chocolate—although the varieties are endless. Cinnamon, cloves, aniseed, coriander, and even peanut butter can be found in mole recipes.

Preparing fresh mole sauce is easy: Sauté about 3 cups of finely chopped onions and 2 large cloves of pressed garlic in vegetable oil until golden brown. Add the following ingredients: 2 cups chicken broth, 3 tablespoons chili powder, 2 teaspoons sugar, 2 tablespoons cocoa powder, and 2 tablespoons peanut butter. Simmer for about 20 minutes.

Experiment by adding any of the above-mentioned ingredients, such as cinnamon or coriander. I use peanut butter, although the traditional recipe calls for ground peanuts. Added to chili, mole brings a unique Mexican flair and added sweetness. When using mole sauces in chili, be sure to compensate heavily for ingredients that are already in mole, or use just enough to "sweeten" your chili.

Masa Harina

Masa harina is Mexican cornmeal, developed by Quaker Oats through a Mexican government program aimed at saving their citizens a few hours a day from making tortillas the old-fashioned way. Masa harina is used traditionally for tamale and tortilla making, so the flavor's an appropriate one for chili. Chiliheads use a tablespoon or two to thicken up and "tighten" watery chilis. The wonderful tortillalike flavor adds even more authentic southwestern flavor to traditional beef chilis. Be careful not to use too much, or you'll feel like you're eating sand.

Broths

For any chili recipe that requires long simmering times in a liquid (which is most of them), you can replace water with broth. Chicken or beef broth adds tremendous flavor to meat that is simmering, but again, don't use too much. Usually, if a recipe calls for 6 cups of water, I replace 2 of them with broth. I prefer to use low-sodium broth and season to taste at the end with table salt—canned broths pack a tremendous (and unnecessary) salty punch.

Vinegar

When making rice and beans, try putting a tablespoon of good vinegar in the mix prior to serving. The tangy acidity helps break down that "starchy" flavor. A dash of vinegar added to tomato-based chilis has a similarly beneficial effect.

Sweeteners

Having a sweetener in chili is key to balancing the fire of the hot peppers while bringing out the other flavors of the spices. Properly sweetening chili is a balancing act. Too much sugar, and you have dessert; too little, and you have turpentine. If you are making chili for six, as most of the recipes in this book call for, the minimum amount of sugar you should use is 1 full tablespoon.

You don't have to limit yourself to white sugar. Brown sugar, honey, molasses, and even chocolate can be added to give your chili a tinge of sweetness. My friend Buck's recipe calls for "a liberal squirt of Log Cabin" syrup! For those of you who abhor anything sweet near your chili, try using cocoa powder or a dash of cinnamon for balance.

Chapter Four
The Recipes

Beef Chilis

In this section I've tried to include a well-rounded selection of traditional and "fancy" beef chilis. The first two recipes are what I'd consider "basic" Texas-style chili—recipes from which all your future chili concoctions can spring. There's also an "authentic" chili con carne recipe, which adds some tomatoes. In honor of the great state of Ohio, second only to Texas in terms of chili obsession, I have included a recipe for Cincinnati-style chili—a baroque adaptation served "5 ways." In addition, you'll find some fancy recipes demonstating that anything (and nearly every ingredient you can think of) is appropriate for chili.

"Original" Texas Chili

You want to make some real, authentic Texas cattle-drive chili? This is your recipe, and one you can use as the basis for all future chili recipes and general experimentation.

You make this recipe the old-fashioned way, using fresh ancho chiles (and maybe a tepin or two, if you're feeling frisky) and real lard. There are no tomatoes in it—this "bowl of red" gets its color from cayenne pepper and paprika, both members of the *Capsicum* genus. Every chili recipe you'll make is basically a variation on this simple theme. Over the years, peppers and onions have found their way into the skillet, as well as many and varied spices, including prepared chili powder. But this is about as authentic as it gets. You can serve this to a Texan in a 10-gallon hat without any worry.

6 ancho peppers

1 dried chipotle pepper

2 tablespoons rendered beef kidney suet

2 garlic cloves, minced

3 pounds lean stewing beef, cubed into ¼-inch pieces

1 teaspoon leaf oregano

1 tablespoon cumin seeds, ground

1 tablespoon cayenne pepper

1 tablespoon paprika (for color)

2 tablespoons masa harina

Reconstitute the dried chile peppers as described in chapter 3, reserving the pepper water for use later. Get a hot skillet going and add the suet. Sear the beef cubes in garlic until brown on all sides, about 5 minutes. Add the pepper water until it covers the beef by an inch. Reserve any remaining pepper water, as you may need to add some later. Bring the mixture to a boil.

Reduce the heat and simmer for 45 minutes. Add the rest of the ingredients, except the masa harina, (which you'll use at the end as a thickener) and the chipotle pepper (which you'll use to adjust the heat). Cook the chili for 45 minutes to an hour, or until the beef is fork-tender. Add additional pepper water as the liquid evaporates, keeping the beef well moistened. Check for thickness, and add masa harina as necessary. You want this chili to stand up on its own—with about the same pourability as a newly opened bottle of Heinz ketchup. Check for heat. If it's not hot enough, add the chipotle pepper. Simmer the mixture for another 30 minutes.

Serve with nothing. No rice, no beans, no crackers.

Guests are allowed to skim the fat off the top if so desired.

Serves 6

Another "Original" Recipe for Texas-Style Chili

There are probably as many "original" Texas chili recipes as there are places that serve chili in Texas. The recipe below transmogrified over the years, and turned into my personal conception of what true Texas-style chili should be (hot, greasy, thick, and red.) The "red" should come from chili powder, not tomatoes. It should be made from cheap meat and simmered long enough to make that meat tender, but with a bit of texture to it. You should be able to taste it afterward, via highly verbal belches, for about 12 hours. It *should* also be prepared with real suet or lard, but that's where I draw the line. I substitute bacon for lard and leave it at that. I have enough problems in my life—cooking with lard doesn't have to be one of them.

4 strips extra-thick bacon

3 medium onions

10 small garlic cloves

4 pounds boneless beef chuck, trimmed and cut into ½-inch pieces

⅓ cup chili powder (mild to medium hot, depending on taste)

1 tablespoon ground cumin

5 cups water

2 teaspoons dried oregano

2 teaspoons salt, or to taste

1 tablespoon sugar (not necessary, but I like it)

1 tablespoon masa harina

2 teaspoons cayenne pepper

First, you'll need to generate your suet substitute. That means bacon. Fry up a few slices, reserving the bacon grease in the pan. Eat the bacon. Immediately add your onions and garlic (chopped, not pressed!), and cook until the onions are soft, about 5 minutes. Add the beef and cook until it's slightly browned on the outside, about 4 minutes. Now add the chili powder and cumin, being sure to stir well into the mixture.

Add enough water to cover the mixture, and bring to a simmer. Add the oregano and salt. Cover. Simmer for several hours until the beef is fork-tender (between 1½ and 3 hours, depending on how tough the meat is). Right before it's done, add the sugar (if desired) and the masa harina. Stir until slightly thickened, about 5 minutes. This chili is about 10 times better after it sits in the fridge for a few days, but it usually doesn't last that long.

Serve with a dollop of sour cream and finely chopped onion—or sliced scallion—on top.

Serves 6

Chili Con Carne

Chili con carne literally means "chili with meat." Making this chili the traditional way means keeping it simple. I make the concession of adding a bit of tomato paste and paprika for flavor and color, and a small dose of sugar to offset the spice. This recipe is a great starting point for numerous variations, so feel free to add vegetables and spices at will— you just can't mess this one up!

2 tablespoons vegetable oil

4 garlic cloves, finely chopped

1 large onion, chopped coarsely

3 pounds cubed beef

2 tablespoons ground cumin

5 tablespoons chili powder

2 teaspoons salt

2 tablespoons paprika

⅛ teaspoon cayenne pepper

1 (6-ounce) can tomato paste

4 cups water

1 tablespoon dried oregano

1 tablespoon flour (optional)

Sugar, to taste (optional)

1 tablespoon dried oregano

Get your skillet or Dutch oven hot and add the vegetable oil. Sauté the garlic and onion until soft, and then add the cubed beef, cooking until slightly browned on the outside. Add your spices and tomato paste, stirring well. Add the water and bring to a strong simmer for 15 minutes.

Reduce the heat to medium low and simmer until the beef is tender—about 2 hours. You should have a thick and hearty consistency at this point. If it's still watery, use flour to thicken it up. I like to add about a tablespoon of sugar right before serving.

Serves 8

Black Bean Ancho Beef Chili with Avocado Salsa

This is a doctored-up chili con carne, served with a refreshing avocado salsa on the side. I like to prepare this with freshly ground beef if possible. If you don't have a grinder, ask your butcher to grind some fresh beef to the correct proportions (about the width of your pinkie). This is key, because you don't want your meat to dissolve into minuscule bits in the pan, making it dry and without texture. You can skip the molasses if you like, but I think it adds some thickness and balances the hot pepper. It also complements the black beans.

For the Chili:

½ pound (about 1½ cups) dried black beans

¼ cup vegetable oil

2 large onions, chopped (about 3 cups)

1 tablespoon chopped garlic

1 red bell pepper, chopped

3 pounds boneless beef chuck, coarsely ground

1 tablespoon ground cumin

2 tablespoons paprika

3 ounces (about 6) dried ancho chiles, diced (stemmed and seeded)

1 tablespoon crumbled dried oregano

1 tablespoon dried hot red pepper flakes, or to taste

1 (28-ounce) can pureed tomatoes

3 tablespoons cider vinegar

2 tablespoons unsulfured molasses

⅓ cup chopped fresh coriander

For the salsa:

1 avocado

1 large tomato

½ cup finely chopped red onion

1 pickled jalapeño, seeded and minced

1 teaspoon fresh dill

1½ tablespoons fresh lime
juice, or to taste

Salt and pepper, to taste

Prepare the salsa:

Peel the avocado and dice it into ½-inch sections. Slice the tomato
in half and remove the interior, leaving the flesh. Dice the tomato into
squarish, ½-inch sections. Add the chopped onion, jalapeño, and dill.
Add the fresh lime juice and stir. Let stand for approximately 10
minutes before serving to let flavors mix. Add salt and pepper to taste.

Prepare the Chili:

First, soak your beans by covering them completely with water for about
an hour. Drain them and set aside. Put your skillet over high heat and add
the vegetable oil. Sauté the onions, garlic, and bell pepper until slightly
browned, about 5 minutes. Set aside. Add some more oil to your pan and
sauté the beef until browned. Drain the excess fat and put the cooked
vegetables back into the skillet.

Add the cumin, paprika, chiles, oregano, and hot pepper flakes. Stir until
thoroughly mixed. Add the canned tomatoes. Bring the mixture to a simmer
and add vinegar, molasses, and black beans. Simmer for 20 minutes. Add the
coriander and simmmer an additional 10 minutes, about 15 minutes before
serving, reserving some to sprinkle on top of the dish. Serve with salsa on the
side and tortilla chips.

Serves about 6.

Cincinnati Chili

If you're going to eat in a real Cincinnati chili parlor, you have to know how to order a proper bowl of chili. You can order it "3-way" (chili over spaghetti, with shredded cheese on top and oyster crackers on the side); "4-way" (add onions on top); or "5-way" (the whole nine yards, with beans). I like it "6-way," with a heaping dollop of sour cream! With the exception of the bed of spaghetti, which I find somewhat odd, I am a tremendous fan of Cincinnati-style chili—and you will be, too.

4 large garlic cloves, pressed

2 large onions, chopped

1 quart water

2 pounds ground beef

1 (16-ounce) can tomatoes

1½ teaspoons white vinegar

1 teaspoon Worcestershire sauce

2 tablespoons chili powder

2 teaspoons ground cumin

1 large bay leaf

1½ teaspoons ground allspice

1½ teaspoons salt

1 teaspoon cayenne pepper

1 teaspoon ground cinnamon

Cooked spaghetti—enough for 6 servings

On the Side

Shredded Cheddar cheese

Oyster crackers

Chopped onions

Kidney beans

Sour cream (not "official"!)

In a large skillet or Dutch oven, sauté the garlic and onions in hot lard (or vegetable oil with a tablespoon of butter added). Add water until simmering. Add the beef. (You will actually be boiling the beef, instead of sautéing it, but that's the way they do it in Ohio, I guess.) In go the tomatoes, vinegar, Worcestershire, and all of the spices. Simmer for 3 hours. Serve to your guests "3-way," leaving the onions, beans, and sour cream on the side. (The cheese always goes on top; there is no "2-way" chili served in Cincinnati!)

Serves 6

Jen's Chili

This is the chili I've been making for years, and the one my wife likes the best. It's a standard chili con carne dressed up with peppers and scallions. Whenever I cook the more "traditional" Texas-style chilis, Jen just isn't that impressed. I can see her point—why settle for less by eating a plain bowl of chili when you can add tremendous flavor using beans and fresh vegetables? Her Italian background also demands I substitute olive oil for lard and add lots of fresh garlic. But with the exception of a teaspoon or two of adobo I stick in, this really could be characterized as a "healthy" chili dish.

¼ cup olive oil

2 large onions, chopped

3 scallions, diced

1 tablespoon chopped garlic

3 pounds boneless beef chuck, cubed into ¼-inch pieces

¼ cup good chili powder (I like Gebhardt's or Pendery's)

1 teaspoon adobo

1 tablespoon ground cumin

1 tablespoon dried oregano

2 (8-ounce) cans tomato sauce

1¼ cups beef broth

3 tablespoons cider vinegar

1 teaspoon cayenne pepper

1 (19-ounce) can light red kidney beans

2 green bell peppers, chopped

2 red bell peppers, chopped

Get your skillet hot and add a generous amount of olive oil. Sauté the onions, scallions, and garlic until softened, about 5 minutes. Add the meat and sauté until it's browned on the outside, about 5 minutes.

In go your spices: chili powder, adobo, cumin, and oregano. Cook, stirring well until the spices are fully integrated into the mixture, about 2 minutes. Now add the tomato sauce, broth, vinegar, and cayenne pepper. Simmer uncovered for 1½ hours or until the beef is fork-tender (it may take longer, depending on the quality—or lack thereof—of the chuck). During this time, the chili should be reduced to a nice, thick consistency.

Add the beans and bell peppers during the last 15 minutes of simmering and cook until the peppers are tender.

Serves 6 (4 if I'm there)

"Commander" Tim's Submarine Chili

By Tim Coleman

Serving chili aboard a submarine might sound like a recipe for disaster. Beef and beans, enclosed spaces—you do the math. I'm here to tell you otherwise. Back in 1990 I learned my friend's father was an ex-navy man who served for months at a time on a U.S. sub. I also found out he doubled as the cook. His favorite meal to make for the crew was chili. His recipe was simple: He took what he had and put it into one big pot. Everything that came out of that pot went into one big bowl—bread included.

For us landlubbers, Sub Chili makes a great dish and it's easy to fix. Whip up a batch, call some friends, and rent a double feature—*The Hunt for Red October* and *Crimson Tide*, maybe. If it's good enough for the men and women in uniform, it's good enough for the rest of us.

3 medium garlic cloves, minced

1 medium onion, chopped

2 tablespoons vegetable oil

1 pound ground beef

2 cups water

1 (8-ounce) can tomatoes

2 tablespoons chili powder

2 tablespoons paprika

1 teaspoon ground cumin

1 teaspoon salt

2 teaspoons cayenne pepper

1 teaspoon sugar

2 cups corn

2 cups red kidney beans

½ pound Cheddar cheese (cubed)

Rolls or crusty bread

3 squirts Tabasco per bowl

On the Side

Only a cold drink and a spoon; a napkin if you're lucky. (Remember, those are some tight quarters on submarines.)

In a frying pan, sauté the garlic and onion in vegetable oil. Mix in the beef. Pour in water until it's simmering. Add the tomatoes and seasonings, including sugar. Simmer for 1 hour. Dump in the corn and kidney beans. Simmer for another hour. Add the Cheddar cubes and simmer for 15 more minutes. Place a roll or crusty slice of bread in each bowl. Pour chili over the bread.

Shoot 3 squirts of Tabasco on top of each bowl. Give to your guests and pop in the first tape. Who's got the remote?

Serves 4 hearty souls, or 2 Navy SEALs

(Tim Coleman is a sometime chef and full-time writer whose work has appeared in *Playboy* and other publications; he's currently writing a novel. He lives in New York City.)

Four-Alarm Chili

Why "four-alarm" chili? Well, this refers both to the chili's inherent heat and to the fact that more chili is consumed in American firehouses annually than in the rest of the entire industrialized world. One local fireman here in New York explained that a four- or five-alarm chili is so called because of the amount of time it takes to cook it: "Five-alarm" recipes should simmer for about as long as it takes to extinguish a blaze of that magnitude, while "one-alarm" recipes can be prepared in the time it takes to douse an oven fire. He may have been pulling my leg, but I call this recipe "four-alarm" chili because of the four fiery ingredients I use to give it heat: Tabasco sauce, pickled hot peppers, cayenne pepper, and a habanero.

10 strips extra-thick bacon

4 pounds beef round steak, cubed

2 large onions, diced

1 large green bell pepper, diced

4 garlic cloves, minced

1 quart beef broth

1 (28-ounce) can tomato purée

1 cup water

6 tablespoons chili powder

2 teaspoons ground cumin

1 teaspoon ground oregano

2 teaspoons cayenne pepper

1 (4-ounce) can pickled hot peppers

1 habanero, stemmed, deseeded, and chopped

1 teaspoon Goya *sofrito*

4 vigorous shakes Tabasco (or other hot pepper sauce)

1 (12-ounce) can black beans

1 (12-ounce) can red kidney beans

½ cup masa harina

Salt and black pepper, to taste

Fry the bacon until crisp, crack open a cold beer, and start eating the bacon. In the pan (leaving the reserved bacon grease), brown the cubed beef. Add the onions, bell pepper, and garlic. Sauté for about 5 minutes, until the vegetables are softened. Transfer to a large pot and add the liquid ingredients: beef broth, tomato purée, and water. Stir well, bringing to a simmer. Add the spices, chile peppers, *sofrito*, and Tabasco. Cook for 2 to 3 hours over a low flame. Add the beans and masa harina (for thickening) about 20 minutes before serving. Adjust the seasonings with salt and black pepper to taste.

Serves 8

Grilled Rib-Eye Chili

There's nothing better than a perfectly grilled rib-eye steak fresh off the grill. And when I can get away with it, I save steak leftovers to make sandwiches, or I add them to chili. This recipe is kind of a conglomeration of an excellent dry-rubbed steak and a regular type of chili. My friends think I'm crazy to "waste" a beautiful piece of prime aged steak in a bowl of chili. But if you like steak and you love chili, the combination is awesome.

For the Steak (Dry Rub):

1 teaspoon ground cumin

1 teaspoon chili powder

½ teaspoon kosher salt

½ teaspoon coarsely ground black pepper

¼ teaspoon cayenne pepper

For the Chili:

2 large rib-eye steaks, grilled (about 3 pounds)

¼ cup olive oil

2 large onions, chopped

3 scallions, diced

1 tablespoon chopped garlic

¼ cup good chili powder

1 tablespoon ground cumin

1 tablespoon dried oregano

2 (8-ounce) cans tomato sauce

1¼ cups beef broth

1 teaspoon cayenne pepper

1 (19-ounce) can dark red kidney beans

1 (12 ounces) can black beans, rinsed and drained

3 large red bell peppers, chopped

For the Garnish:

8 ounces sour cream

2 tablespoons prepared horseradish

1 medium chopped red onion

Mix the dry-rub ingredients together in a bowl and rub the mixture into the 2 steaks. Place in a sealed plastic bag overnight. Grill your steaks until rare (or broil in the oven if no barbecue is available). Let them cool and slice into ½-inch pieces, trimming any excess fat. Set aside.

Prepare the chili according to the instructions on page 56 (Jen's Chili) without sautéing the meat. The sliced steak is added during the last 5 minutes and cooked to your preferred doneness (for rare, about 5 minutes; medium, about 10, and so on). Mix the sour cream and horseradish and add a dollop to each dish. Sprinkle some chopped red onion on top.

Serves 4

Poultry Chili

Even hard-core chili addicts will settle for a nontraditional bowl of red—but only if they have to. The following recipes offer a good substitute for beef chili, and can be surprisingly healthy. Try substituting lean turkey meat for ground beef to make a tasty "white chili." For true lovers of the chile pepper, nothing is better than a chili that accentuates its fresh flavor by highlighting the pepper itself rather than the meat.

Turkey Verde Chili

Although turkey chili can be delicious, you wouldn't be caught dead showing one at the annual Lexana, Kansas, Chili Cook-Off. Still, there's something to be said for a bowl of chili that's not rimmed with grease—at least, once in a blue moon.

I got this "verde" recipe from my friend Jim, whose 300-plus cholesterol count forced him to reassess his twice-weekly chili habit. There are no tomatoes and no grease, just an abundance of fresh-tasting green onions and chiles, cilantro, and moist, white turkey meat.

2 tablespoons vegetable oil

16 ounces turkey breast strips, cut into ½-inch-long strips

2 tablespoons masa harina

2 teaspoons ground cumin

1½ cups chopped green onions

2 cups (or more) canned low-salt chicken broth

½ cup canned diced green chiles

½ cup chopped fresh cilantro

Place your skillet on the stove over high heat and add the vegetable oil. When the oil is hot, add the sliced turkey and sauté until golden brown, about 7 minutes. Reducing the heat, add the masa harina and cumin, coating the turkey meat. Continuing to stir, add the green onions and sauté until slightly softened. Add the chicken broth and chiles. Simmer for 10 minutes. Right before serving, add the cilantro.

This dish can be served over white or brown rice. I like to drizzle it with a little bit of flavored extra-virgin olive oil to make up for the lack of grease in the recipe. Try using a spicy pepper oil—easy to make yourself or available at your local gourmet store.

Serves 4.

Thanksgiving Chili

Here is my take on a classic turkey chili—simple to prepare but elegant enough for a Thanksgiving meal, at least if it were up to me and not my wife. Remember to watch those cooking times when cooking poultry chilis—unlike chuck beef, which benefits from long cooking times, turkey will get stringy and tough if overcooked.

5 ounces (about 6) dried ancho chiles, diced

3 cups water (reserved from chile peppers)

8 cups turkey, cooked and diced (breast meat)

4 tablespoons salted butter

1 elephant garlic clove

   (or 4 large regular garlic cloves)

2 medium red onions, chopped

4 large celery stalks, diced

2 (12-ounce) cans low-sodium chicken broth

2 (28-ounce) cans stewed tomatoes

1 (4-ounce) can tomato paste

2 tablespoons paprika

1 tablespoon ground cumin

1 tablespoon crushed oregano

1 ounce piquin peppers, diced

Cayenne pepper (as needed to adjust seasoning)

2 (12-ounce) cans dark red kidney beans, rinsed and drained

1 (12-ounce) can corn

Salt and pepper, to taste

Prepare your chiles as discussed in chapter 3 (see page 22). Prepare the turkey by boiling turkey breasts in salted water until thoroughly cooked (about 15 minutes, depending upon the size of the breasts).

Heat the butter in a large skillet or Dutch oven (the larger the better, as you're cooking a huge batch) over a high flame. Sauté the garlic, onions, and celery until golden. Add the chicken broth, tomatoes, tomato paste, soak water, peppers, and spices. Bring the mixture to a boil, stirring well. Check for heat and add 1 teaspoon of cayenne pepper if necessary. Reduce the heat to a simmer and add the beans and corn.

Simmer for approximately 20 minutes, until thickened. About 5 minutes before serving, add the cooked turkey. Adjust the seasonings with cayenne pepper, black pepper, and salt. Serve over rice with warm buttered rolls on the side.

Serves 10-12

White Chili

White chili is the exact opposite of a true Texas-style bowl of red. First, it's healthy; with the exception of the cheese, most nutritionists would approve. Second, it isn't red—it's clear (or "white"), with beautiful highlights of green chiles and a tinge of red cayenne pepper.

A note on preparing the chicken: Depending on your taste, you can either cube boiled chicken breasts or boil select parts and shred the meat away from the bone. Cubes cut from the breasts add to the pristine nature of this "white" dish, but dark-meat lovers may not care.

1 tablespoon extra-virgin olive oil

1 teaspoon unsalted (sweet) butter

2 medium onions, chopped

2 garlic cloves, finely chopped

1 scallion, diced

8 ounces chopped chile peppers (mild)

1 tablespoon ground cumin

1 teaspoon cayenne pepper

6 cups chicken stock

3 (16-ounce) cans navy beans

4 cups diced cooked chicken, cubed

Salt and pepper, to taste

Fresh parsley

Sour cream

Fresh chives, finely diced

Grated sharp Cheddar cheese

Get your skillet hot, and add the olive oil and butter. Sauté the onions, garlic, and scallion until limp. Add the chile peppers, cumin, and cayenne pepper. Stirring frequently, cook for about 5 minutes. Add the chicken stock. Simmer for 30 minutes.

Add the beans and precooked chicken and cook for another 15 minutes, or until the chicken is heated through. Adjust the seasonings with cayenne, salt, and pepper. Add parsley. Serve over rice with a dollop of sour cream and grated Cheddar cheese on top, decorated with fresh chives.

Serves 8

Tucker and Maggie's Grilled Corn and Chicken Chili

Last summer Jen and I were hanging out with our neighbors, Jon and Joy, sipping margaritas and barbecuing. I was grilling some corn and chicken, and planned on serving it with a rice and vegetable dish. As I brought the tray of barbecue into the kitchen I saw that my four-year-old English cocker spaniel, Tucker, and his friend Maggie, a four-year-old cocker-mutt, were polishing off the last grain of rice. They'd managed to knock the dish off the kitchen counter and figured they might as well clean up after themselves.

As luck would have it, I had a quart of leftover 3-bean chili in the fridge. I popped it in the microwave, sliced the chicken, took the corn off the cob, and mixed it all together. Voilà! Grilled Corn and Chicken Chili—one of my favorites, and ridiculously easy to prepare.

4 large chicken breast cutlets, trimmed

4 cobs corn, shucked and cleaned

2 tablespoons balsamic vinegar

2 tablespoons vegetable oil

1 large onion, diced

2 green bell peppers, seeded and diced

2 garlic cloves, minced

1 jalapeño pepper, seeded and minced

1 (28-ounce) can crushed tomatoes

2 tablespoons chili powder

1 tablespoon dried oregano

1 tablespoon ground cumin

1 teaspoon paprika (sweet)

1 teaspoon salt

½ teaspoon ground black pepper

Cayenne pepper to taste (substitute hot pepper sauce)

1 cup red kidney beans (rinsed and drained)

½ cup black beans (rinsed and drained)

½ cup navy beans (rinsed and drained)

Prepare the Corn and Chicken:

Pound the chicken cutlets until approximately ½ inch thick, rub with a light coating of olive oil, and season with salt, pepper, and chili powder. Grill them over high heat for about 5 minutes on each side until cooked through. Parboil the corn for about 5 minutes and transfer to the grill, cooking for approximately 5 minutes.

Slice the grilled chicken into ½-inch pieces and put in a large bowl. Using a sharp knife, remove the grilled corn from the cob and place in the bowl with the chicken. Pour the vinegar over the corn and chicken, stir well, cover with plastic wrap.

Prepare the 3-Bean Chili:

Heat the vegetable oil and sauté the onion, bell peppers, garlic, and jalapeño until soft. Add the canned tomatoes and spices. Reduce the heat and simmer for 20 minutes. Add the beans, chicken, and corn and simmer for an additional 10 minutes.

Serves 4-6

Pork, Sausage, and Other Meats

Chili made with our friend the pig can be very tasty indeed. How about lamb chili? Excellent. Duck? Absolutely. Chili is one of the few dishes that can accommodate a wide variety of meats—or none at all. I hope the following recipes will give you some "food for thought" the next time you take that long stroll down the meat aisle in your supermarket. Maybe there's something you can do with those oxtails after all!

Heartland Pork Shoulder Chili

Man can't survive on beef and poultry alone. Pork has been making a slow but steady comeback over the last decade as more people realize just how healthy and flavorful it can be. Like traditional beef chilis, this recipe leverages the cookability of a lesser cut of meat—in this case, a boneless pork shoulder—to withstand the long cooking process. I like to get my pork from R&S, the local purveyors of pork. They consistently deliver a fresh and well-trimmed portion. If your neighborhood isn't blessed with a similar store, your local butcher at the supermarket will have to suffice.

3 pounds boneless pork shoulder, well trimmed

Flour

Olive oil

2 medium onions, chopped

3 large garlic cloves

4 poblano chiles

2 serrano chiles (or dried japones)

1 large can stewed tomatoes

2 (19-ounce) cans enchilada sauce

1 cup water (substitute beer or chicken broth)

1 tablespoon ground cumin

2 tablespoons chili powder

1 teaspoon cayenne pepper (or to taste)

First, prepare the pork shoulder by trimming it and cutting it into 1-inch cubes. Moisten the cubes with water, shake off excess moisture, and dredge in flour. Get your skillet nice and hot, add an ample amount of olive oil, and brown the pork on all sides over a high flame for approximately 7 minutes.

Transfer the pork to a bowl, leaving the remaining oil in the pan. Add more oil if necessary, and quickly sauté the onions and garlic until golden. Add the chiles, canned tomatoes (I prefer to use whole stewed tomatoes and chop them in the pan to get larger pieces, but you can purchase chopped tomatoes), enchilada sauce, water, and spices. Simmer while stirring frequently for about 45 minutes, or until the pork is fork-tender.

Serves 8

Black Bean and Chorizo Chili

This chili dish incorporates two of my favorite foods: *frijoles negros*, flavorful black beans, and *chorizo*, the spicy Mexican sausage. Chorizo is wonderful, as it will crumble into bite-sized pieces perfect for chili.

My good friend Alberto made me this dish when I was visiting him in San Andres, a beautiful farming community in Mexico about two hours south of Veracruz. We ate large batches of this chili with rice and cold bottles of cheap Mexican beer. Delicious!

2 tablespoons olive oil

2 ½ pounds chorizo sausage

2 large onions

1 large red bell pepper, diced

1 large green bell pepper, diced

3 large garlic cloves, chopped

4 jalapeño chiles, diced

3 tablespoons chili powder

2 teaspoons ground cumin

1 tablespoon crushed oregano

½ teaspoon cayenne pepper

½ teaspoon crushed red pepper flakes

2 (28-ounce) cans crushed tomatoes

6 ounces Tecáte (or any Mexican beer)

3 (12-ounce) cans black beans

First, cook the chorizo in olive oil in a large skillet over medium-high heat for about 10 minutes. Transfer the chorizo to a plate, and sauté the onions, bell peppers, garlic, and jalapeños for about 5 minutes until soft. Add the chili powder, cumin, oregano, cayenne pepper, and red pepper flakes, stirring well. Next, add the canned tomatoes, beer, and beans. Slice the chorizo into bite-sized pieces and add. Simmer over medium-low heat for about 15 minutes.

Serve over rice. Garnish with sour cream if desired.

Serves 2

Kickstand Willy's Pork Shoulder Chili

My good friend William got the nickname "Kickstand Willy" on a camping trip a few years back, celebrating the end of a mutual friend's bachelorhood. Usually a gentleman in every sense of the word, Willy found himself a bit under the weather one morning, after consuming ungodly quantities of Pabst Blue Ribbon beer and bourbon.

I found him around six o'clock in the morning, standing in two feet of water. He was asleep, held aloft by an oar that was propped into his stomach, giving him the appearance of a tilted bicycle leaning on its kickstand. We let him sleep that way for about an hour before carrying him to a tent to recuperate. Unfortunately, no pictures were taken.

This is the chili I made for Willy and the gang that night, which is uniquely suited as a hangover cure. As a tribute to Willy's unique sense of balance, I added some bourbon and beer to the recipe.

8 ancho chile peppers, chopped

1 chiltepin pepper, stemmed, seeded, and blended

6 slices bacon

4 pounds pork shoulder, cubed into ¼-inch pieces

5 garlic cloves, pressed

3 medium onions, diced

1 green bell pepper, chopped

1 red bell pepper, chopped

1 can Pabst Blue Ribbon (or similar cheap beer)

2 ounces Old Times bourbon (or similar)

1 small can tomato paste

3 cups pureed tomatoes

½ teaspoon allspice

¼ cup ground cumin

2 tablespoons brown sugar

2 tablespoons Tabasco sauce

Masa harina (if necessary)

Salt and black pepper, to taste

Remove the stems and seeds from the ancho and chiltepin chile peppers and chop finely. Set aside. Fry the bacon in a saucepan or Dutch oven large enough to hold the chili. Eat the bacon, or save to add it on the side, crumbled, to your chili.

With the bacon fat still in the pan, brown the pork shoulder pieces for about 10 minutes, turning often. Remove from the pan and set aside. Add oil, and sauté the garlic, onions, and bell peppers until soft. Now add the beer and bourbon, and bring to a boil. When boiling, add the chile peppers, pork, tomato paste, tomatoes, spices, cumin, and sugar. Reduce the heat to a simmer and cook for 1½ hours, stirring frequently. Adjust the seasonings with salt, black pepper, and Tabasco. Thicken, if necessary, with the masa harina.

Serves 6-8

Lamb Chili

Lamb chili is like a gourmet highball of pure delight. Tender, rich lamb shank and real chile peppers combine with a hint of rosemary and traditional chili spices to create a dish that would be as comfortable in a Park Avenue apartment as on the dusty trail. Some supermarkets sell ground lamb meat, which is more than adequate for this recipe—albeit somewhat tender, so avoid overstirring it! The better move is to ask your butcher to grind you some fresh shank meat, a tougher cut that's more suitable for the rigors of chili cooking.

2 tablespoons extra-virgin olive oil

1 large green bell pepper, diced

1 large red bell pepper, diced

2 large onions, chopped

8 garlic cloves

2 pounds lamb shank meat, ground medium width

4 New Mexican peppers, chopped

4 de arbol peppers, chopped

1 (28-ounce) can chrushed tomatoes

1 small can tomato paste

16 ounces low-sodium chicken broth

2 ½ teaspoons cayenne pepper

2 ½ teaspoons ground cumin

1 (19-ounce) can red kidney beans, rinsed and drained

Salt and black pepper, to taste

Place a large skillet over high heat and add enough oil to coat the surface well, about 2 tablespoons. Sauté the bell peppers, onions, and garlic until translucent, about 8 minutes. Add the lamb meat and sauté until browned, stirring occasionally.

Prepare the chile peppers according to the method described in chapter 3 (see page 22) and add. Sauté for an additional 3 minutes and reduce the heat to medium. Add the crushed tomatoes, tomato paste, broth, and spices. Bring to a rapid simmer and reduce the heat to low. Simmer for 45 minutes. Add the beans and simmer for an additional 15 minutes, until heated through. Adjust the seasonings accordingly with salt, black pepper, and cayenne pepper. Garnish with fresh rosemary.

Meatless Chilis

Although I consider myself an unrepentant carnivore, occasionally I like to eat "healthy." One of my favorite healthy dishes is vegetarian chili. Start with the basics—chiles, garlic, onions, cumin—and then let your imagination run wild. Fresh carrots, celery, scallions, bell peppers, zucchini, squash, and—of course—beans can be combined in almost any configuration to create a delicious chili. And if you really love the flavor and sting of real chiles, there is no better way to taste them than in a bowl of meatless chili.

One of the best things about preparing meatless chilis is the preparation time. Because you don't have any meat to tenderize through slow cooking, most recipes can be started and finished in less than 20 minutes. I have included three excellent meatless recipes: a basic five-bean chili, a black bean vegetable chili, and a wonderful lentil chili. All of them can be modified, depending on your taste, by substituting or adding different kinds of beans and vegetables.

Five-Bean Chili

Although I specify five beans for this recipe (black, navy, pink kidney, garbanzo, and red kidney), these are just my personal favorites. Try using pinto beans, black-eyed peas, or any other bean you can think of. And come to think of it, why stop at five beans? Try adding 7 or even 10 different varieties! Legumes are the "meat" of the vegetarian world, adding bulk and subtle texture to a variety of meatless dishes. If you love beans, you will love this chili.

For the Chili:

2 tablespoons olive oil

2 large onions

3 garlic cloves

2 medium carrots

2 medium zucchini

1 green bell pepper

1 celery stalk

1 (28-ounce) can pureed tomatoes

1 teaspoon ground cumin

2 tablespoons chili powder

White pepper

Cilantro

Salt and black pepper, to taste

½ teaspoon dried oregano

6 ounces black beans

6 ounces navy beans

6 ounces pink kidney beans

6 ounces garbanzo beans

6 ounces red kidney beans

Salt and black pepper, to taste

For the garnish:

Grated sharp Cheddar cheese

Scallions, chopped

Sour cream

In a large skillet, heat approximately 2 tablespoons of olive oil. Coarsely chop the onions and garlic, and sauté until soft. Dice the carrots, zucchini, and celery and sauté for an additional 5 minutes. Add the tomatoes, cumin, green pepper, oregano, chili powder, and white pepper and bring the mixture to a simmer, stirring frequently. Simmer for 20 minutes. Add the beans and cook until heated through—about 10 minutes. In the final minute of cooking, add some chopped cilantro. Season with salt and black pepper to taste. Sprinkle with diced scallions and grated sharp Cheddar cheese, and add a dollop of sour cream.

Serves 10.

Black Bean Vegetable Chili

This recipe calls for 5 ounces of mild chiles. New Mexican, ancho, pasillas, or Anaheim chiles are perfect, either alone or blended together. If you can't find dried chiles, you can substitute 2½ tablespoons of chili powder in the recipe.

2 tablespoons olive oil

½ tablespoon butter

1 celery stalk, diced

1 large white onion, chopped

1 elephant garlic clove

1 medium green bell pepper, chopped

1 medium red bell pepper, chopped

5 ounces mild chiles (diced or pureed)

2 tablespoons ground cumin

1 tablespoon dried oregano

16 ounces pureed tomatoes

4 cups black beans

Cayenne pepper, to taste

Salt

Heat the olive oil and butter in a large skillet and sauté the diced celery, onion, and garlic until soft. Add the green and red bell peppers, the chiles, and the spices and sauté an additional 5 minutes.

Add the tomato purée and bring the mixture to a simmer. Stirring frequently, cook for approximately 15 minutes. Add the beans and cook until heated through, about 5 to 10 minutes. Adjust the seasonings and heat with cayenne pepper and salt. (If you're using dried, reconstituted chiles, you can add a cup of reserved pepper water at the same time you add the tomatoes.)

Serves 4-6

Lentil Vegetable Chili

One of the better vegetarian chilis I've had, this recipe harnesses the awesome flavor of lentils. Long a staple of Middle Eastern cooking, lentils make for a great meat substitute in chili and are easy to cook—it takes as little as 20 minutes for the dried lentils to soften.

There are several varieties to choose from, but the ones you will most often find in your local supermarket are European lentils, which are light brown. Red and yellow lentils can be found in specialty food stores or Middle Eastern markets, and may be substituted, depending on your taste.

2 tablespoons olive oil

1 large onion, chopped

3 large garlic cloves, pressed

4 medium scallions, chopped

1 red bell pepper, chopped

1 green bell pepper, chopped

1 large carrot, peeled and diced

1 (28-ounce) can pureed tomatoes

2 medium dried ancho chiles (stemmed and deseeded)

1 small chipotle chile (stemmed and deseeded)

1 cup reserved pepper water

8 ounces lentils

2 teaspoons ground cumin

2 teaspoons dried oregano

White pepper

Cayenne pepper

Salt

Low-fat sour cream

Sauté the onion, garlic, scallions, red and green bell peppers, and carrot in olive oil for approximately 7 minutes, or until the onion is translucent. Add the tomato purée and the stemmed and deseeded chiles. Bring to a simmer over medium heat. Add 1 cup of the water you used to reconstitute the dried chiles. Bring back to a simmer and add the lentils, cumin, and oregano. Cook for 20 minutes, or until the lentils are soft. Adjust the seasonings with white pepper, cayenne, and salt. Serve with a dollop of sour cream on top.

Serves 6

Chili Resources

You can't become a real chilihead just by reading books—it takes years of practice, and lots and lots of bowls of chili. I hope I've taken you a few steps down the path to becoming a true chili aficionado. Even after years of making all kinds of chili, there's a lifetime more to learn and thousands of recipes to taste.

If this book whetted your appetite for chili knowledge and lore, you can delve into the following resources to find everything you ever wanted to know about America's favorite dish—and then some.

Chili-Related Reading: A Selected Bibliography

A Bowl of Red
Frank X. Tolbert
Texas A&M University Press

Published in 1966, Tolbert's fascinating book is, for many aficionados, the Holy Bible of chili. An in-depth look at the history of chili, its origins, legends, and modern-day lore, *A Bowl of Red* will tell you more than you ever wanted to know about your favorite food. Hard to find, but try some used-book sellers at Amazon.

The Great Chili Book
Bill Bridges
The Lyons Press

You want some intense chili arcana? Look no farther than *The Great Chili Book*, published in 1981 by Bill Bridges. Offering "101 variations on 'The Perfect Bowl of Red,'" and an even better history than Tolbert's, this book was appropriately called "manna for advanced chili addicts."

While I'd consider the book you're reading now "Chili 101," Bridges, a much more senior professor of chili, gives the graduate-level "Chili 400" class. He includes recipes for all the "original" chilis, such as pemmican chili, Wick Fowler's chili from the first Terlingua cook- off, and LBJ's "Pedernales River Chili." Contact The Lyons Press at 1-800-243-0495 to see if they have any copies lying around.

The All-American Chili Book: The Official Cookbook of the International Chili Society
Jenny Kellner and Richard Rosenblatt
Hearst Books

This is ICS's official chili cookbook. It contains 28 winning cook-off recipes (until 1994), and recipes from celebrities and other chili notables such as Bill Clinton and Roger Clemens. The only drawback is the lack of photographs, but I guarantee you'll be happy with any of the award-winning concoctions.

The Chile Pepper Encyclopedia: Everything You'll Ever Need to Know About Hot Peppers
Dave DeWitt
William Morrow and Company

Want to know more about chile peppers? Dave DeWitt's fascinating *Chile Pepper Encyclopedia* leaves no stone unturned in its quest to catalog every single chile pepper in the world, and provides practical information on heat and usage. You may use only a fraction of the peppers he lists, but this is the reference to have on hand when you're ready to gain an intimate knowledge of chili's principal ingredient. Try the chipotle sauce recipe—it's amazing.

Chili on the Web

If you live in the Northeast as I do, good luck finding poblano peppers and Pendery's chili powder. You'll likely have to settle for canned jalapeños and McCormick's (not that it's so bad)! That's when I turn to my computer and do my shopping on the Web.

How about finding that perfect recipe for "firehouse" chili, or tips on freezing chile peppers? Here are some Web sites you will find extremely helpful for your chili-making adventures.

Pendery's
www.penderys.com
1-800-533-1870
Fax: 214-761-1966
E-mail: penderys@mindspring.com

Here is where you can get the original "chilomaline" powder Pendery brought to Texas in 1870. You can also choose from a wide variety of "capsicums," chili blends, and spices—basically, every single authentic ingredient you'd need to make Texas-style chili. Most impressive are the dozens of available varieties of ground chile powder, from the basic (de arbol) to the obscure (tres ochos). While you're there, be sure to order the largest size package of chilomaline powder you can find.

Chile Head
http://easyweb.easynet.co.uk/~gcaselton/chile/chile.html

This amateur site is a repository of literally hundreds of great chili recipes, facts about chile peppers, and, according to the site, the "largest chile variety database in the world!" Run by "chilihead" Graeme Caselton out of the United Kingdom, Chile Head puts a tremendous amount of chili and chile information right at your fingertips. Check out the excellent tips on preparing and canning chile peppers.

Pepperfool

www.pepperfool.com

Tel: (818) 953-5062

Email: RobL@PepperFool.com

Another site for the chile pepper fanatic, Pepperfool has interesting links to various chili-related sites and an even better listing of chile pepper purveyors. If you're into growing your own peppers, this site has more than a dozen resources for acquiring chile pepper seeds and some great growing tips. You can order dried and fresh chiles and order some excellent hot sauces directly from the site as well. The books section provides a comprehensive listing of chile-pepper-related titles.

International Chili Appreciation Society (CASI)

www.chili.org

This site is about as down home as the association itself. You can get a glimpse at this year's CASI Cook-off winner, as well as the award-winning recipes from years past. Want to join the society or put on your own official CASI cook-off? All the details are here. I love checking out the photos of the winners on the site—this is what true chili-heads actually look like!

International Chili Society (ICS)

www.chilicookoff.com

The ICS has been around since the beginning. In fact, the famous first "official" chili cook-off took place on the land of one of its board members, Caroll Shelby, the famous car racer and designer of the Shelby Cobra sportscar. Since 1967, charities have raised more than $65 million through ICS-sanctioned chili cook-offs. That's a lot of chili.

Want to put on your own officially sanctioned ICS chili cook-off to support your favorite charity? This site shows you how. Don't forget to check the recipes section, listing all cook-off winners, including the original recipes from Wick Fowler and H. Allen Smith's duel in 1967.

The Ring of Fire: Fiery Food Website Neighborhood
http://www.ringoffire.net

While not chili-specific, this Web "ring" (a collection of sites that agree to link together to promote each other) focuses on hot foods—mostly those that get their heat from chile peppers. There are loads of goods commercial sites (for private-label hot pepper sauces and the like); some great commercial Web sites (Pepperfool is one); and fun amateur sites (like the "House of Pain"— http://members.tripod.com/~Gkhan/hse-pain.htm—dedicated to "culinary skydiving and mouth surfing with capsaicin"). It's worth it to take a lap around the Ring, if only to remind you just how bad the early days of the Web were!

ACKNOWLEDGMENTS

First of all, there is no way I could have written this book without the support of my publisher, Tony Lyons, who provides a tremendous amount of encouragement in the form of e-mails, royalty statements, and the occasional lunch at The Tonic. Brando Skyhorse, my editor, is also to be thanked for his skillful editing and patience with my last-minute manuscripts.

Willie Nash also requires special acknowledgment, as he is so much more than the photographer of these books. Willie test-cooks all the recipes prior to shooting them, and does a tremendous amount of work developing and perfecting the recipes. Also included here is my wonderful wife, Jennifer. An excellent cook in her own right, she helped turn a sheaf of scribbled recipes into a chili book worth reading, and never complains about having her kitchen transformed into a chili laboratory for several days a month. A special thanks is owed to Graeme Caselton, whose passion for chile peppers helped inform several chapters of this book.

Index